Locutions

Locutions

Susan McCaslin (signature)

Susan McCaslin

Ekstasis Editions

Canadian Cataloguing in Publication Data

McCaslin, Susan
   Locutions

   Poems.
   ISBN 0-921215-88-6

   I. Title.
   PS8555.O87M87   1995   C811'.54   C95-910224-8
   PR9199.3.C67M87   1995

© Susan McCaslin, 1995
Cover artwork: Miles Lowry, *"Between the Worlds"*.

Acknowledgements
Some of these poems have appeared, or are about to appear, in *Bellowing Ark, White Wall Review, The Kore, Anima: The Journal of Human Experience, The Journal of Feminist Studies in Religion, Moksha Journal,* and *Descant.*

I would like to thank my husband, Mark, for his unfailing support of my writing and for his editorial skill; Hannah Main Vanderkamp, Celeste Schroeder, Janet Allwork and Patricia Stone for the generosity of their friendship; Dale Zieroth for his example; Richard Olafson for his belief in my work; and my daughter, Clara, for her presence.

Published in 1995 by
Ekstasis Editions Canada Ltd.   **Ekstasis Editions**
Box 8474, Main Postal Outlet   Box 571
Victoria, B.C. V8W 3S1   Banff, Alberta T0L 0C0

Locutions by Susan McCaslin has been published with the assistance of the Canada Council and the Cultural Services Branch of British Columbia.

Printed and bound in Canada by Hignell Printing, Winnipeg, Manitoba.

CONTENTS

The Wisdom Poems — 7
Prelude — 9
She Stands At The Mall — 10
You Will Have Plain Speech From Me — 11
Those Who Love Me I Love — 12
Her Path Is The Path Of Justice — 13
I Was Fashioned In Times Past, In The Beginning — 14
I Was Playing In The Presence — 15
Watching Daily At My Threshold — 16
All Who Hate Me Are In Love With Death — 17
Wisdom Has Built Her House — 18
But Wisdom Was Beyond My Grasp... — 19
You Do Not Know How A Pregnant Woman... — 20
Before The Silver Cord Is Snapped... — 21
The Use Of Books Is Endless — 22
For My Radiance Is Unsleeping — 23
She Enters Into Holy Souls... — 24
I Am A Spirit, Subtle, Free-moving... — 25
Moving More Easily Than Motion... — 26
Like A Fine Mist I Rise — 27
She Is The Brightness That Streams — 28
Flawless Mirror Of The Active Power — 29
She Makes All Things New — 30
Temperance, Prudence, Justice and Fortitude — 31
In My Friendship Is Pure Delight — 32
First Of All Created Things — 33
Her Yoke Is A Golden Ornament — 34
Let Your Feet Wear Out Her Doorstep — 35
Stalk Her Like A Hunter — 36
Worship Is The Outward Expression Of Wisdom — 37
The Wise One Is Silent Until The Right Moment — 38

Songs Of The Beloved — 39
The Song Of The Shulamite — 41
Esposa De Lebanon — 42
Poetic — 43
A Garden Enclosed — 44
Summer Reading — 45
Beloved, Unnumbering The Stars — 46
A Poem In Which The "I" Disappears... — 47
The Marriage Of Wilderness And Poetry — 48
Poetry To Wilderness — 49
Poetry To Wilderness II — 50
Hieros Gamos — 51
Difference — 52
Aphoristic Love — 53

On The Beloved's Navel	54
There Is No Word More Beautiful Than Spouse	55
My Beloved Is To Me Sweet	56

The Angelology 57

Angel Descending	59
Annunciation Angel	60
Snow Angel	61
Polar Bear Angel	62
Magnolia Angel	63
Warrior Angel	64
Human Angel	65
Posting Angels	66
Poetry Angel	67
Guardian Angel	68
Death Angel	69
Wrestling Angel	70
Light-Burden Angel	71
Angel Of The Stolen Children	72
Fruitful Angel	73
Circumambulatory Angel	74
Greening Angel	75
Seraph Angel	76
Holocaust Angel	77
Polysemous Angel	78
Music Angel	79
Watching Angels	80
Cherubic Angel	81
Altar Angel	82
Unicorn Angel	83
Symmetry Angel	84
Book Room Angel	85
Angel Ascending	86
Evolution Angel	87
Energy Angel	88
Wheel Angel	89
Stocktaking Angel	90
Cloud Angels	91
Naked Angel	92
Bird Angel	93
Pure Angel	94
Teleological Angel	95
Angel Descending (II)	96

The Wisdom Poems

For Mark

Prelude

Wisdom came with a face
of turquoise conjured eyes
to which I held up a great
roll of print on metal plates
being ground out constantly
by the media depicting
child abuse break-ins murders
rape gang wars kidnappings
torture disease starvation
riots bombs interrogations
etcetera glut information over
load of our times with words
and images produced and controlled
by something definitely not human.

What can I do
but be caught up
in all of this?
What can I do?

Make your mind a contrary plate.
Order your own reel of words and images.
What is full of me cannot be impressed upon
by another.

Come home first. Then my doing will start.
This is not an admonishment.
Because you asked.

She Stands At The Mall

face pale and round as the moon.
She is Wisdom, Hokhmah.

There is judgment in her name
but not the kind you expect.

She is God and her hands beseech.
She is woman and she laments

on the hill by the open gate.
She sits like a heron,

pilaster chiselled in dusk.
Displaying herself in the half-light

where people throng to shop
she seems to have something to offer.

She could be a whore
with her heart a sachet of incense,

but you have mistaken her again.
She is virgin—not the kind you want.

Distilled, pressed out, she keeps
her power unbroken.

Her eyes are a colour
you have not invented.

They seep from so many places.
She is speaking, appealing.

Listen.
She appeals now to so very few.

You Will Have Plain Speech From Me

Metaphor bore me.
But for you I have stripped all adornment.

I am dancing in the play of language.
I am dancing the world alone.

You help create me, but I precede you.
You precede yourself to me.

Why do you not know me?
I am not morality, not a crackable code.

You cannot break me, or measure up to me.
I am not law, though my feet obey.

I transcend ethics, but you must comprise
the ethical to get me.

The main thing for you to remember is this:
teeth full of money and pockets of power

suffice for the time.
But there is something you've forgotten.

There is something you lack
better than red coral, gold, amethyst—

expensive dust. Believe me.
There is a currency you need.

Those Who Love Me I Love

I am dying but I do not die.
I am a migratory bird,

endangered peregrine,
flying to your receptive spaces.

There in your dark I will nestle.
Promise.

Her Path Is The Path Of Justice

But who would demand justice
knowing her inexorable, blindfolded,

unbiased? In cold light
we are all doomed to come up short.

Then she removes her mask,
folds in her violet scarf

the scarred hands of the Argentine pianist
detained, mutilated for nothing.

To her breast cleaves the raving girl,
raped by her father and his cronies

for nothing better; laves with unguent
the native boy betrayed by his priest,

cleanses those who were never unclean,
returning the guilt to the guilty.

Then out over ravaged forests,
sweeping down the clearcuts in glacial ice,

she removes the removers, withers
their incentives, investments at a glance.

Can we believe the wrong way will perish?
If we cannot ask for her justice,

let us hope for her mercy.
For judgment is mercy rejected.

I Was Fashioned In Times Past, In The Beginning

Think ballerina stars—
then throw them back into a point.

Think sea—
then meld it to the stars,

let it swallow the moon and sun,
let it shimmer as it devolves to mire

and a small sucking sound, a single cell
perfect in its finite way.

Think earth, springs, mountains, hills,
pockets of incensed air, pine needles erect

whirring into a vortex—white dwarf.
Then in that utter silence

long before past was what you call past
imagine me, leafless, twigless,

pregnant with myself,
pregnant within creative spirit,

single, before the fecund blast
danced out of the unformed

into what you see—blue camas, manzanitas,
blue-eyed Marys, sea-blush,

lavender shooting stars, coral root, orchids—
a thousand islands floating across time.

I Was Playing In The Presence

The problem is you have forgotten how to play.

You do not enjoy yourself enough.
Let me tell you a story.

Say it to yourself—"I play
therefore I am."

One and one—make one.
You and the divine.

You enter, creative,
clash cymbal and drum,

design pleasant stigmatas
for your feet and hands.

I never wanted torture.
Make your colours breed.

Let your words revel into dark
and out again. Then what?

The presence has moved on.
You were all that—there is more.

God is beyond you—yet you know God.
You and God are partners in that dance.

Watching Daily At My Threshold

If two spotted fawns dance out of a glen,
(you perspiring after an arduous hike)

appearance, apparition—take them as a gift,
a kind of unexpected grace.

But if I, Wisdom, should come at evening
to one who makes prayer habitual,

rising or sitting, waiting for me
not too seriously, but seriously enough,

knowing that such visitations require discipline,
know that I will not disappoint that one.

My door opens of itself,
springing back a little on its hinge.

All Who Hate Me Are In Love With Death

They do not know me, unpatternable beauty,
yet they hate with indifferent hate,

battening on death like black flies,
dismembered parts, body parts.

Harmful, they mean bodily harm,
sucking in, devouring the gifts.

Why invert the dance to non-dance,
twisted gymnastic of the lost people?

Why court the love-drained Courtier?
Come away from the fields of rue

to the meadows of praise, love-trod
where there is only one gambol.

Wisdom Has Built Her House

The other side of monster-mega-homes
on cramped suburban lots where instant

neighborhoods arise for instant profit,
Wisdom, with a carpenter's saw and plane

has smoothed her cedar, set cleverness
in the foundation, perspicacity in the frame,

wit in the joins. She has withdrawn
her hands and finished with "a little

night music," installing herself
as she builds out of laughter

a house to outlast times, seasons.
Just outside the strip mall, beyond

the grease of quick burgers and fries,
she has laid her table, spiced her wine.

But Wisdom Was Beyond My Grasp, Deep Down, Deeper Than One Can Fathom

Who am I to speak of holy Wisdom
with my headaches and complacencies?

Yet once, she dropped a locution
on my lap. Once I glimpsed her

between the bank and Zellers
without scarves, nimbus, robes,

plain really, but with such a look.
Before that I thought heaven

something outside, beyond belief,
to be stepped into or not

depending on contingencies. Now it is
what I build with her or not

span by span across deep space
on the tracks of her treading.

You Do Not Know How A Pregnant Woman Comes To Have A Body And A Living Spirit In Her Womb

So much goes on without you,
at least the part you call you.

You are not, after all, the measure
of all things, pivoting there

through your own procedures, modus operandi,
driver's manual to the stars.

Only I know how two bubbles
join with a third rejoicing voice.

You could have willed dark
and the light would have continued.

Even as the body and spirit geometrize
music, sinking their charts deep

in the DNA, I am absorbed, creating
what will come out of you.

Before The Silver Cord Is Snapped And The Golden Bowl Is Broken

remember me. You are facing emptiness
not death. Just what you failed to imagine.

Every snap is a break, luck for you,
if you know how to use it.

The reins at the back of your neck
are silver cords that have rested

in the hands of significant angels.
The bowl that is your body's

deepest thought, empties its wine
beyond grief and beyond measure

where I, God's exiled female self,
catch in my hands your golden secret.

They say you have conjured me
out of dust to palliate despair.

But what is this voice,
draped in the cloth of your being?

The Use Of Books Is Endless

which is to say nothing against books
rather that the intellect rolls

out its endless print, ungrateful
to the lacunae, blanks breeding light.

I am resplendent in your silences—
drink me in—eat me—let me be

and I will return your scroll of words
shining. Be literate for what means.

God and I will piece together stories
scattered in your palimpsest bones.

What you need is not so far away.
You are the book you lack, each missing page.

For My Radiance Is Unsleeping

alert as a child at the third level of sleep
when dreaming stops and the body

rocks in its chariot of stars,
and angels (discussing what to do)

sift their fingers through your hair.
Then I awake who have never slept,

(all my being an active repose)
God-Sabaoth saying, "It is good."

From your centre I move outward,
activate your central, unblinking eye,

study circumference, detaching each
unreal desire till it rests.

I would give you in a moment
what you laboured at for years.

When will you wake with me to dance
in the light that returns "*magnus deus*"?

She Enters Into Holy Souls, And Makes Them God's Friends And Prophets

I speak for the deconstructed soul
whether whole or unwhole,

the integral self you raze
and raise out of moth wing and flame.

The question is not so much
"Does God exist?" as "To what

do you open?" when you find yourself
stranded, standing on nothing.

Mostly I enter when you have lost
yourself, your old god-words—

bringing to your eyes before you,
prophet, a more profitable way.

God is not distanced then, her,
his, spirited laughter spilling

over bells and pomegranates
at the fringe of your robe.

Just because your categories
do not hold, I am within you.

I Am A Spirit Subtle, Free-Moving, Lucid, Spotless, Clear, Invulnerable

and I see only one, not two trees
blooming in that primal park

made over in industry's image
into highrise towers, corporations

protected by bombs, poisons, nerve gas.
So it was not for most, my wisdom tree,

and they banished themselves from its shade
to go where they would be less

discomfited by the sparks blown
from my eyes called "an angel's sword."

But my tree did not consume itself,
or go away, or simply die.

The phoenix still sings in its leaves,
all in all, all acting in all,

whether or not they are feeling,
thinking, listening—growing green.

How long will they resist my sparks,
fountain, seed? How long

will they desiccate the tree
scattered in the brain, heart, genitals?

Moving More Easily Than Motion
I Pervade And Permeate All Things

pure decree newly issued from the mouth,
guest resident in pileated woodpecker,

tree frog, bald eagle, garry oak
arbutus, island within island dreamed.

And if I hook you by claw or talon,
branch or piercing twig, giving you over

for an instant to the power of right
discernment, a kind of uncommon sense

or skill to walk your sterile streets
in a guise or mask shaped by me,

the means and end of your walking
will never be separate. The fear

of what you can do or not do
is only the beginning of me.

Like A Fine Mist I Rise

They have called those who love me
schizophrenic, for I speak in so many voices,

anonymous but never mute, muted.
Vocal with riddles I burn

in the phoenix-heart, building
and shattering your names for me.

I am mist lifting, brooding
on opening texts. I conserve

by making everything new,
justify myself in your deeds.

My locutions are strung pearls,
all radiant, perfectly shaped.

When the memory is hardly working
they fall distinctly on the ear.

She Is The Brightness That Streams

and I the obfuscated mirror
unreflecting, till her kindling words

send me back into the world.
Because of her I am in the writerly way,

fructified by the streaming
that amends suburban nights

vaulting one who is scriptless
into worded unbroken act.

Flawless Mirror Of The Active Power

Technology could be hazardous to your health
and further economic growth uneconomic.

Unemployed ghosts with triggered fingers
lurk in the shadows of your machines.

Malign computer screens, clock dials,
hairdryers could do you in, or someone

hatter mad in the unforgiving dark,
stalking through malls randomly

spraying death. How can you walk
if I mirror your cracked world?

Who will go with me down
where the active power wrests

from the restless-forgiveness—
me, auroral, coming through glass?

She Makes All Things New

In another tale of her telling
you are fleeing the paramilitary

when you stumble on an antique map
of burnt-out towns, parchment

curling slightly on its edge.
Wisdom points where it cracks,

peels back to show earth's undergreen;
roads and markers, bas relief

relieves the sense of being lost.
You only thought it was the end.

Re-entangled with the webbed stars
and minted earth you go to meet what comes.

Temperance, Prudence, Justice And Fortitude

maiden aunts and virgins, all
smelling of lavender and rosewater

cast off their crinolines and pose
for the journal of interconnectedness.

We have heard of you but not tasted
your virtues. Temperance hangs

her balance in the air—a kind of
golden section, proportionate;

Prudence, uncareful, thrusts herself
between the junkie and his fix,

while Justice justices, and Fortitude
taking her sisters' hands, strips off

the last vestiges of force.
They circle in Hokhmah's face

calling all poets and dreamers down
to build on their jewelled floor.

In My Friendship Is Pure Delight

but despair, inaction, distraction
keep you from clasping my hand,

me from clearing your room
to make a sacred space.

Where in your cheques and balances
is there place for my light

housekeeping, the measureless
spoons of my honey?

First Of All Created Things

you are always first and last
with your repertoire of good tricks,

bag-lady madonna haunting the fringe,
conjuring what is old and new

from suburb or hub, spoke or wheel.
When you were spoken and first spoke

did our ears come spiralling?
Will you visit us again

when we surpass this transformation,
these falling warehouse walls?

Her Yoke Is A Golden Ornament

worn lightly, royally
when she yokes herself to you

foolishly, unevenly, in service
of the one. There are after all

only two roads—one up, one down.
But on the upper road you fly.

Let Your Feet Wear Out Her Doorstep

To get her drops, sink into the humus
of her garden. Grow veridical.

Fraternize with wind and sun
though they grow grave.

Surely she will take pity on you,
tame her wildness and open the door.

The flow from that fissure
will break and mend your heart.

Stalk Her Like A Hunter

but softly—for she proliferates
and will not be netted in your nets.

She is language gone wild, meaning
expanding, subtle as grass.

When you think you have her
she vanishes; yet a residue remains,

heart-hum ready to compose
sonnets for Armageddon.

Worship Is The Outward Expression Of Wisdom

Though no one is falling
at her feet, she throws herself

into your whirlpool, absorbing
the kidnapped, slaughtered innocents,

the raving witless traders in despair.
There is in her a fertile abyss

that takes your roll of print
(sins stamped on air,

the worst that can happen happening)
and swallows it whole.

You may be stripped down
but there is nothing outside her.

Even in emptiness
there is somewhere to stand.

The Wise One Is Silent Until The Right Moment

I sound your spurious dreams.
What vexations fly from your box

of words, images, solicitations?
Court me, but if I propose

silence, wed me in solitude.
From that cloister sing out the timely word.

Songs of the Beloved

"And when you make the inner as the outer, the outer as the inner, and the upper as the lower, and when you make male and female into one, so the male shall not be male and the female shall not be female, then shall you enter paradise."

The Gospel of Thomas

The Song Of The Shulamite

Nard, myrrh and cinnamon
drip from my twin-fawn breasts

that have nourished and released
so many star-flung children.

I am swarthy from too much sun
but I have survived melanoma.

I have claimed and danced my rage.
I have seen Christ knocking

at the door of the churches
and watched him go away into the night.

I know what it is to stand at a door
pressing the bell to distraction.

I am not an allegory of the bride
though I weave and unweave my veils.

My enclosed garden is not virginity
but a sacred space where I write.

I am sealed off, open only to openness.
I make books and armies,

but not for bloody war.
I am Eternal Female in space

but in time I have been both male and female.
When God the Androgyne divides

I and my love rock in volcanic fissures.
His and her answering metaphors

blow the suburbs to smithereens
then to a human shape.

Esposa De Lebanon
(or I'd Rather Make Love in Spanish)

My husband is a gardener
but most he loves the wild.

My spirit is an androgyne,
a broken piece of God.

The psychological claptrap
that most consumes our age

is to the child who orders me
a pile of blissful dust.

"Esposa" is a lovely word
sounding best in Spanish

as *"cara mia"* in Italian
improves on cold "my dear."

I am disordered most in June
when peonies arrive.

I am beloved first in God
who knit me in her womb.

Beloved to our counterselves
beloved in the Bride

we bless and then are eloquent
in this exquisite night.

Poetic

God is in love with language
that points and is dumb

in love with paradox—
the cryptic, gnomic phrase

in love with sound and silence,
what can and cannot be said,

but sick to death of language
in love with its own cleverness,

in love with minnows streaking down
under a mirroring stream,

a few words held as dictated.
The strain of recording exactly—

then standing back.

A Garden Enclosed

faltering into light
the pale green tarragon
mint and reeling lavenders
mouth a honey sun.

Spears of fierce irises
brace for release.
Moribund peonies
sigh magenta rose.

Naked fingers
lift perennial bulbs
brush off flakes of sod.
Push them deeper down

down to rising time.

Summer Reading

Endless summer rain seeps
like indelible white ink
into the spine of a book
open in the middle

just at the place
where the lovers kiss

plummeting past
the indecipherable watermark
their bodies made

where the story's other end
meets the edge of the page.

The book goes up—
conflagration fanned to gold.

The lovers are fishing
the book from the stream,
drying its damaged leaves in the sun,
tracing with their salt lips
its broken colophon.

Beloved, Unnumbering The Stars

Who counts
my purse of eggs
my bag of tears
dropping one by one
into time's thicket?

Each egg lost in its tear-pool
each tear circled by its star

I cannot impose my order on the world
or even guide my rich, unnumbered eggs' careen.

A Poem In Which The "I" Disappears Only To Return At The End Chastened And Pure

I

could not look upon the ground
it so transfigured me

(the feminine in all slumbering in all)

oh wind-burned bush
leaning into the lake

I

The Marriage Of Wilderness And Poetry

The old-growth cedar's
ceremonial coupling with sky,

the osprey's elliptical path and plunge
into a parting emerald lake,

the aviary branches' smooth embrace
receive us in this swooning sacrifice.

Poetry To Wilderness

I didn't find you in books.
The sounds you made were not

plod or trudge across a page
to make the bright mind buzz

but turning, cooing. Sleepily
I felt your chiselled face.

I did not crib you from texts.
Your cataracts fell into me.

At once I ceased to affect you,
ceased efforting. Refused completely

to hold myself up anymore,
write myself in or out,

would rather hear you say,
"Attend, attend to the osprey's

ingenious claw, the curve of her
ebony beak, her laser eye."

Your voice dropped another line:
"God doesn't care if you catch fish,

only that you dive into this flow."

Poetry To Wilderness II

I didn't find you through reading.
The sounds that brought you

were not linear.
They did not plod or race across a page
but cooed like doves
or moaned sleepily
turning over and over
in their cells.

I didn't crib you from texts
or lectures, you fell over me,
water's drape,
altering every word.

I was empty.
I was nothing again.

You said wildly,
 "Attend this osprey
in his crazy plunge.

God doesn't care
if you catch fish
or speak of fish.
Just send them back,
honouring."

Hieros Gamos

A whole anthology of fireweed
        a lexicon of phlox
gloried, outspilled

"and the earth helped the woman."

Difference

If I were a man
I would have no hips and walk naked.

As a woman
I prefer my breasts tangerines
under a poet's ruffled shirt.

Aphoristic Love

My body memorized your body
like the timetables.

My body memorized your body
as if my life depended on it.

O, for a short compendium
of the dreaming body,

not for the best
that has been thought and said

but for a short history
of the dreaming, abridged mind,

abbreviated for the nonce
like foolscap compressed

into yellow wafers.
One taste, and suburban refugees

might become (if not whole)
at least addicts of the holy.

On The Beloved's Navel

world-hub, honeyed grail,
centre, sinew, spun

peach skin, fuzzed dip,
under-pulse's heart

where the cupped ear reaches
back

There Is No Word More Beautiful Than Spouse

cara, mi esposa.
No honey-dripping sound
at the door more laden
more lovely
than spouse.

My Beloved Is To Me Sweet

as a lolling word
lallation on the tongue
la la
lollapalooza

that heady banquet
spiced spray

The Angelology

For Claire

*"This world, seen no more with human eyes
but in the angel, is perhaps my real task."*
　　　　　　　Rainer Maria Rilke

*"Everything is conducted by Spirits,
no less than Digestion or Sleep."*
　　　　　　　William Blake, *Jerusalem*

"All is by mediation."
　　　　　　　Philo Judeaus

Angel Descending

Flaming
(incandescent)
out of the superflux
a frond floats
(plumed, pinioned)
into the heart of an enclosed
suburban garden.

A peri (periphrastic)
visits my window.
I do not entertain wings
yet they blow in
fierce as hippogriff's
or griffin's, resting lightly
on the turned earth.

Annunciation Angel

This time she surpasses
her biological prime.
So many mouths encumber earth.

Her mysterium tremendum
will not vex her age
with another birth.

Vellum slips from her hands.
The lectern slants
its light onto marble.

The pale lily straightens.
In a feathering breeze
the messenger enunciates

transparency, fine linen
and silk, hyacinthine,
scarlet and true purple.

She remembers angel food
cake when she was three,
foresees what her weaving

will cover and unveil
then plunges again
with her "How shall this be?"
into the angel's "Hail!"

Snow Angel

How you spread
the wealth of yourself before us in snow,
limning the tips of trees
fantastical castles' filigree.

We surmise wings
pressed in the drift,
white on white on dazzle gold,
catch you pivoting on the upslope.

Yet you slip into us
from below the snowline
through the corner of the eye
into the heartmelt,

send steam rising
through every pore.

Polar Bear Angel

Who is to say she (in all her stuffed mortality)
does not lumber over Bethlehem
pausing to caress the Christ Child,
then zoom back to Santa's workshop
just in time for Christmas;

that she has no remarkable voice
that no luminous companion flickers
in her cracked, flecked eye?

My daughter tells me when she furs you
love migrates from her body into yours
and hibernates inside you all winter.

Who am I to linger outside belief?

Magnolia Angel

astir, compacted in bud
or loosened from the twig
in tincture of rose-to-white
fleshy aromatic petals.

How easily
you unwing yourself before us.
Only a brief fluttering
gives you away.

Warrior Angel

I have too long evaded you,
put you off to marginalia,
you with your dragon-trampling feet,
your wings dripping vermilion.

I did not call for protection.
Michael, your hairs are not saffron
but burnished mahogany, and your hands
crossed over your hilt, ebony.

Which came first, you or the icons?
You do not bring personal messages
of comfort and consolation.
The cherubs scatter before you.

What warrior maiden in me rises
to meet you at the crossing
where there are still some things
worth your kind of fight?

Human Angel

You are the one who goes and returns
in fire and morning chatter
over oatmeal and newsprint.

In your eye's heart a window
opens and the stars fall in,
periodically disclosing more

comfort than you know, eremite.
You bewilder my wildernesses.
A thousand campanulas ring

tintinnabulation in our small
talk. Solid, you walk beside me
where Thrones, Dominions whirl

our days into an upward vortex
over the iced green grass
and home to our warm bed.

Posting Angels

What matter
insubstantial,
wheels out of inner
space, terrified
at its nerve?

What diamond
breaks through the roof
grinding crystal out
of our advanced
dread, despair?

What letters
carried post-haste
fly at our doorsteps
though we leave them
unopened?

Who said they
were pretty or
safe, they who transcend
us by burning
inside us?

When we least
call or ask they
advance to our need
despite our light-
warding hands.

Poetry Angel

The coal has lain
so long on your tongue,
you are fire.

Even in our chill reception
you lay yourself open,
thinking our no longer
private thoughts.

Scarved in colloquies
you unbind yourself,
butterfly-out-of-zinnia.

Someone, somewhere
will write you out,
exhaustless one,

recapitulating us
who stammer out your word.

Guardian Angel

Your wings could be
embossed with lilies,
festooned across paradise.

Instead you sit quietly
under my child's white
canopy, a wild hawk

with brown mottled wings
curved invisibly into
the arc of your back.

As you gaze through her face
into the face of God,
you work to temper effulgence,

which she, turning,
feels as a light dream.
You tenderly lift her hair,

place a sapphire in her brow.
Your milky breath loosens her limbs
and she sails out into the virgin air.

Death Angel

You of strange provenance,
how you are scaled in me

(hierarchical) always before,
order of my bones.

Always you cloud yourself
so I cannot see your face,

original obscurant. I feel you
are very young, almost beautiful,

walking in my refusals,
waiting for me to catch hold,

let go into your other side.
How you watch my arrival,

refusing adoration, flight.
Azrael of the veils,

cover my body with your million eyes
before the hour of my death.

Wrestling Angel

They say when two of you
make love, head to toe
conjoining fires,
you wrest from air
incorporeal hallelujahs.

Ours is a denser closing
outside your heat and light.

Except when suddenly
my husband's thigh melts gold
against my bone, and you
move between us, grappling
third, assumed in our discourse.

Light-Burden Angel

Tired of meeting with talkers
in love with their talk

I run yellow lights
to collect my light burden,

queenly just-five who, whining,
insists she is not tired—never tired.

Though I am mostly tired, needing
sleep, aching to be alone for 40 days,

to wrap my tent around my golden space
and write my covenantal ark in air.

Yet more, I want her company on this ride,
her chatter, her light breath's shine,

my burden of care that love makes light.

Angel Of The Stolen Children

into whose arms they fall,
who hear the mother's numbed scream

the shredded binding cord's lament,
we ignore you if you come,

blame you if you stay behind.
Where is there sufficient cause?

And when it is over and the bodies found
or not found, where will you brush

your wings to heal us who practice dread?
"If a man offers candy, run screaming home."

Who will explain to the unslaughtered
innocents, their parents' case of nerves?

Fruitful Angel
(for Hannah)

If I were an angel
from the vestibule of mothers
I would amaze you, Hannah,
with a female child tender
as a nasturtium leaf,

drop her on your consoled
breast as God entrusts to the world
all her babes, placing in their hearts
knotted seed spelling love
from her intricate maze.

But because your barrenness is wealth
I will not presume to outguess
the invisible, conceive for you less
than this weight of light, corona
of poems you are bearing, bearing you.

Circumambulatory Angel
(for Celeste)

Pregnant, you would not lie prone,
but ambulatory, strode the malls and parks
all the long week before birthing your twins.

Before they trumpeted themselves on ultra sound
you'd dreamed for yourself an academic gown,
plotted a marriage of theology and the arts.

Now they lie open to your words
absorbing the warm lily
milk that keeps them whole

twin poems blown from a single stem
where the angel you circled
now circles you.

Greening Angel

body's sage hierophany,
who can brush you on canvas,
undiagrammatic, self other
than the self in the self?

Verdure of maidenhair fern,
your body broken for us.
Emeralding fall down sculpted rock.
This is your cup poured out.

Swish of liquid grass
over all the greening world
wrapping in curtaining rain
cedar's voluminous drape.

Seraph Angel

Make us your landscape, burning one.
Brace us with unremitting praise.
Dance illuminations on the borders
of our incunabula. Make us rows
of quaking aspen, careless
green fools for love.

Holocaust Angel

Unsplittable, you never split hairs.
We could mushroom ourselves to Gehenna,
listless from our unlistening.

Still you hang fire, awed, unable
to stop us from ravishing our world,
biting our hands in the afterglow.

I write to you while my husband sleeps.
Is this all word play and foolery
while the neighbourhood divides?

Holograms multiply in your eyes
where a child of the fifties chants,
"Whistle while you work, for Hitler

is a jerk," not knowing who Hitler was
or how tyranny bears itself, how
lampshade eyes, the buried child-skulls

covered over in our youth, burn
under your covering angel hands.

Polysemous Angel

You are the word we most listen for
or do not, the koan we will break
our heads against till we plunge
into your garment's flesh and flow.

Come in, please. Give us a definite
yes or no. Mean one and one thing
only. You refuse. But hand out
seamless shrouds we throw and throw off.

Then you dress us in words we must interpret.
Words that slip and slip, growing wings.

Music Angel

You brandish stars, bend spheres.
But who has heard how deeply
you have sunk yourself in sound?

How your love draws our oh's.
Your binding chords, your roping
lines rest, rest and play.

When I was nine you clapped out
the whole of Beethoven's ninth;
cantatas undulated in my head

as if an orchestra had set up.
Once your voice carved chrysolite,
accompanied by a single violin.

Plato said to copy the Forms.
But who could keep your pace?
Only when you mattered inside me

did your music linger, ambrosial.

Watching Angels

Let's be clear. They are not human.
They are here to serve us, or serve
what is not us. They compose and
discompose us whether we like it or not.

Yet even they cover their faces.
They do not even determine
the direction of their own feet.
They rise at the will of another.

The sacred texts all extend a knot:
someday we are destined to exceed them.
Some of them even now are writing poems
on us, chrysalid ruiners and makers.

It has been made clear. We are not
to worship them, though their most
casual breath could blind us or heal us.

Cherubic Angel

I pillage four-cornered dictionaries for you,
Human, Lion, Ox, Eagle, missing your meteoric
spins, your graceful animal arabesques.

I must eat your sapphire words, then go
simply, simply go into quaternities of silence
if you are ever to show yourself as you are.

I scan the island bay, vigilant for your eyes
disappearing like sleek seal heads just beyond
the threshold of your clean scrolled beach.

Altar Angel

"You must alter yourself.
Without the ritual
of body, song, silence,
there is no power.

By praising you build
your own star ladder.
I wing your heels over
each burnished rung."

Unicorn Angel

Waking, my virgin daughter drinks you
with ambient eyes, drawing in words
for blind me, your vast azure pupils,
a sloping meadow ringed by a city
more towered and emerald than Oz.

"Are there deer, flowers?" I ask.
"Some irises, daisies, no deer,
but running squirrels, one skunk."

"Is the unicorn standing or lying down?"
"Standing by a tree with sharp love
coming from his horn and Jesus eyes."

Symmetry Angel

I am all uneven planes and knots
to your smooth pulse, fluid
superfluity I cannot do without.

Your left arm is under my head;
your right arm embraces me.
Nurse me in your spiralled nautilus.

Slip into my word-strings, mysteries
I name, unname, Seraphim, Cherubim,
Thrones, Dominions, Virtues, Powers.

Bind me together with your non-human
world, your elm arms, bear body,
intrepid comet's flare, dress me

in glory like the virgin's hair.

Book Room Angel

I am in the rare book room
of the university library
shadow to your luminous body

like a vague bride combing aisles
of yellowing manuscripts, watermarked
pages rustling in sororal calm.

The books are veils or curtains,
opaque, then transparent, lining
the dark that absorbs me

into your exquisiteness,
a resonance beyond words, my
scratching pen, fading ink.

I lose nothing of mind and word
if I pass through you,
everything if I do not.

Angel Ascending

We have sought you too much in churches,
erecting walls against the world,
nursing our white moments of lightness.

There is a thick wind on the rim,
a knot in a thunderstorm coming
to blast us all at once alive.

So we enshrine you in tucked sleeves
neatly drawn to the elbow, petit point
folded on a stair you long ago

ascended, you with your thread
of voice rising steadily higher
on our mollusked ear, you

who are not even religious.

Evolution Angel

Swinging around this wounded island
earth, she dives at the word

of another, underground where dream
burrows into vision, planting her gifts

in the rooms prepared for her;
cave or tinctured chamber, four

book-lined walls, diamond apex
cut by Spirit's shaft.

Arcs of her feet grip down
into matrix, mother. Stars

shoot in where there were none.
Brain curls round the pearl

that will survive it.

Energy Angel

In your grammatical universe
I am noun to your verb,
sigil, sign plopped solidly
in bed, my savouring time,
evening time, toys away,
the child asleep, the book
propped on my bent legs,
back pressing your firm.

I am, I need you here.
You salt the night, sing
to breathe, to breathe
entelechy, charging
my words with your
weight of light.

Wheel Angel

You will not be spoken to
or of, you will not
be spoken.

There are you say
no private ecstasies.
You know us.

We should bore you.
So how can you turn
so seriously to include us?

You will not let us pluck
one dahlia by the wall
without you.

You have made us release
the spider from its jar,
ordering its entropy.

Your lips are hermetically
sealed over green eyes.
You, big wheel, insider.

Stocktaking Angel

We aren't nearly out of words
and it is midlife, not critical
really, but time hangs lightweight

on my calcifying shoulders.
You come to take stock, counting
baskets of autumn raspberries.

We have worked; we have been
responsible. And your presence
is surprisingly gentle, whispering

"Well done, and well, it is well
to assess, frame your own horizonless
self that keeps pushing out."

Everything I have said about you
is true and not true. I have accomplished
something and nothing as you slip past

the rags and tags of my speech.
Some things are clear in all this:
You are about language. You care.

Cloud Angels

Highway cruising, she marks
how clouds fold into angel furrows.
Elephants I strain to see
roll (serendipitous) into Beartown.

She wills I never get old,
never go to frostheaven,
and for her I determinedly
grip the wheel

even if only to become
the one she must renounce.

Naked Angel

Yahoos in paradise
keep missing your latest
disclosures.

You crashdived their party
with food in your arms
they would not eat

who swaggered past your
uninterrupted space—
wealthy bankrupts.

Bird Angel

In one of her extravagant self-abandonings
she gathered goose feathers at Como Lake,
brown, grey, lustral white, laughing,
caught gold ribbon in her fingers,
looped it to quill, laced them to her back
so they sat in the joint of her shoulders
just where the muscle tucks in.

Undaunted by gravity she leapt from chair,
windowseat, flapping her narrow arms
again and again, even after being told
"Humans can't fly," reminded of Icarus.
She played the edge for a momentary
suspension of anatomy's disbelief,
trying to recomprise the figure of her dream.

Pure Angel

in your unicorn light
returning everything
thrown at you,

you wedge cuneiform,
scripting my words.
Divine shuttle,

dream carrier, no less
than digestion or sleep,
you bear my sod.

Now in you (transported)
I am first ice
terrible transparency.

There is really nothing
beside you. Not clean,
stardust in snow,

I am given for love;
I am not remembering.
You are too directly

blazed on the brain,
too white through the eye.
Liminal breath, frost, polestar.

Teleological Angel

Without you I dissipate
dust, worm down, curl in

repeat myself endlessly
on some thin edge

tied to no world.
I rant and rave

for you (many, one)
who name yourself

purpose, telos going on
where earth spins

its inside out.
Some see nothing;

some see messengers
everywhere. Just God

weaving her underside:
implacable friend.

Angel Descending (II)

Always deeper through ice
you come melting hearts.

How far, how shamelessly
must mercy unseat herself?

To say we are jackal-hearted,
hyenas, is to vilify

the stunned beasts who scuttle
before our sprawled cities.

Only a thin, broken veil
keeps us from knives in the flesh—

averted eyes to ward off gangs—
only an opal flashlight's

flickering before anarchic dark.
Still you descend the stair

buried in the spiralling spine,
our body's most unlikely speech.